Boundaries *with* Soul

I hope you
find your loving
'NO'
xx
Carly

Boundaries *with* Soul

A Guide to Regaining Control of
Your Time and Truest Values
(without Feeling Guilty!)

CARLEY SCHWEET

Boundaries with Soul: A Guide A Guide to Regaining Control of Your Time and Truest Values (without Feeling Guilty!)

© 2017 by Carley Schweet

Book design and layout by BodyMind Books (bodymindbooks.com)

For permission requests, e-mail the publisher or author at hello@coachingbycarley.com, or send your request to PO Box 91, Fall City, WA 90824.

To contact the publisher, visit CarleySchweet.com

To contact the author, visit CarleySchweet.com

ISBN: 0692855726
ISBN 13: 978-0692855720
(Coaching by Carley LLC)

Printed in the United States of America

To all those who have taught me to say no.

Contents

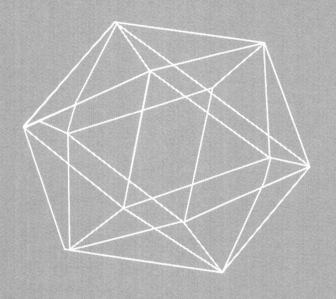

PART
One

We cannot become
what we want
by remaining
what we are.

| Max Depree |

An Introduction

My name is Carley, and I used to be overworked, underpaid, and spread way too thin. I had chronic dry skin on my elbows, itchy patches on my cheeks and eyelids, sleepless nights, and crippling anxiety—the kind that makes your palms sweat and forces you run to the nearest bathroom. On a particularly dreadful day, I found myself locked in the bathroom stall at work, breathing myself through a panic attack. I numbed this pain with nighttime sugary sweets and takeout, almost daily. I drank way too much on the weekends and all too often on the weekdays (Tito's and soda please).

Don't get me wrong; none of the side effects of my not-so-healthy lifestyle were all that bad, but I couldn't shake the feeling that the way I was spending my days and nights felt a bit off. I was stuck between being truly blissfully happy and truly miserable, and my state of being was accompanied by a constant and subtle nagging at my soul. I was comfortable with my life but didn't have passion oozing out of every pore of my being. I was happy but not quite where I thought I could be.

Looking around, I feel like that slightly uncomfortable (but at the same time, all too comfortable) gray area is where a lot of people land these days—within their jobs, relationships, fulfillment, and so forth. Today, we condition ourselves to be okay with merely existing in that gray-area, but we are not passionately in love with our lives. When it comes down to it, a lot of us are happy enough as long as we're making ends meet and showing up to each day with a (possibly forced) smile.

Ultimately, that wasn't enough for me. It's probably not enough for you either.

While living and working in New York City, I didn't realize that I had to take care of myself or that doing so was essential to evolve and become who I am today. I certainly didn't grasp that I could say no to certain people or situations that crossed my path, because telling others no is rude, and I thought that I had to be a yes woman if I ever wanted to get ahead. My days were filled with pleasing others, and it certainly showed. I ended my days exhausted, frustrated, and full of resentment, often thinking to myself,

"Why doesn't anyone care about what I'm feeling?" Humph.

In retrospect, I was blissfully unaware that the chronic boundary violators in my life—the people who walked all over me, demanded too much, and took my niceness as a sign of weakness—might not have cared about how I was feeling at the end of the day. After all, why should they? They had boundaries of their own, and I was probably not voicing that their overbearing behavior wasn't okay with me. Instead, not only did I tolerate it, I smiled through it. And to top it all off, yours truly was the biggest boundary-breaking violator of them all. I broke promises to myself over and over and over again.

Guess what—that shit finally got old.

One day it happened. After dumping my boyfriend of three and a half years, I felt a gentle nagging deep within my soul, and I knew it was time for a major change in my life. I started going to the gym (okay, at first, I was forcing myself to go to the gym) and continued to honor that boundary with myself. Eventually, the time I spent sweating it out became my time, and I learned to say no to the activities that disrupted my precious gym routine. It was liberating. I felt like such a badass, finally being in charge of one hour of my day.

Needless to say, that feeling of honoring yourself, no matter how big or small, is empowering and rather addictive.

Quickly, I found myself building more boundaries—around my time, my emotions, my energy, my food choices, and most importantly, my values—and in turn, these newly discovered limits allowed me to stop people pleasing, take back my time, and focus on what mattered to me.

This process didn't happen overnight. It took me about two and a half years of solid transformational work—visiting personal trainers, overhauling my diet, digging into self-help books, enrolling at the Institute for Integrative Nutrition, and assessing my priorities—to radically feel a shift. Was it easy? No. Was it worth it? Yes.

WHERE I AM NOW

Fast-forward to today: I've become the master of my personal choices and the energy I allow into my life. I quit my corporate job and became a mindfulness-based life coach to help people just like you learn to build boundaries where they need them most. I've learned to recognize my self-worth and encourage mutual respect in every relationship I'm in, and I've gotten in touch with what matters to me in life. Oh, I've also accepted the fact that it's not selfish or rude to do anything that I mentioned above, because honestly, life is too short. Know your worth. Make it clear you'd like others to respect you. Respect yourself. Live according to what matters most to your soul, and trust the process as we work toward bringing your life back to balance.

How are you going to accomplish this? I'll give you one guess.

I wrote this book as a guide for those who are ready to stop living in the gray area according to someone else's rules, those who feel completely stuck and unbalanced, like they're just waiting to fall off the train tracks (or maybe you already have!). I wrote this book for those who want to get in touch with what they truly value, for those who want to get reacquainted with their authentic, truest, highest selves (maybe for the first time!).

I wrote this book for those who finally want to let go of the noes in their lives and say yes to the people and opportunities that matter most. I wrote this book for my "busybodies," the people that are so busy they can't even find the time to eat breakfast in the morning. I challenge you to read this book and see how your priorities shift as you begin to build authentic, real, and healthy boundaries.

Keep reading, please, but only if you're truly ready to shift your life back to balance. It's time for us to start building your boundaries with soul together.

I teach people
how to treat me by
what I will allow.

| Stephen Covey |

Why You're Here

Maybe you're like I was: a twentysomething struggling to make it in a city that's known for being tough on young people and leaving them exhausted, broke, and addicted to sugar (but with a killer closet).

Or it's possible that you're a completely overworked thirtysomething that spends way too much time at the office pleasing others and not enough time with your family. Maybe you're married to a someone who is spread so thin, managing small human lives, a dog, and a three-thousand-square-foot house all on his or her own, with no one to say, "Thanks, you're the best!" or "Wow, we couldn't do this without you!"

There's also a chance that you're a forty- or fiftysomething, fresh off the divorce boat, navigating the daunting dating waters and finding yourself finally getting in touch with what matters to you. Or maybe you're the person that uses food as a reward for a job well done or as a way to cope with your daily stress—never quite satisfying that hungry feeling left within your soul.

There's also a chance you're none of these people, but there's a reason you're here, and believe me when I say I'm so honored you have chosen to show up.

Personally, I think one of the most overlooked (and important) aspects of building healthy boundaries is the connection between your values and your most authentic self. (In this book I also refer to the authentic self as the higher self, ideal self, or intuitive self.)

WHAT YOU MAY GAIN

To create lasting boundaries, we must be in touch with who we truly are at our deepest levels. If this connection with our authentic selves doesn't exist, chances are our boundaries will be built around people, feelings, opportunities, or situations that don't reflect who we are or what we value, making our boundaries easier to dishonor or ignore. Once you start ignoring your boundaries, authentic or not, other people within your life are sure to follow.

The bottom line is that by putting in the effort required and completing this workbook, you'll unlock access to your authentic self and in turn open up the opportunity to create boundaries that feel right to put in place.

One of my most favorite gains from this workbook is the gradual release of anxiety and guilt that many of you may experience as you complete these five steps. Anxiety and guilt are two of the most common side effects for those attempting to build boundaries within their lives, as humans we are conditioned not to ask for what we want but rather to comply with what others expect of us, regardless of whether these expectations are fair or not.

When we find ourselves agreeing with people or situations that don't agree with our authentic and genuine values, an internal dialogue is created, and frequently, we begin to feel anxious or guilty. More often than not, these two feelings alone are enough to stop us in our boundary-building quests. In this pattern of being unquestioningly compliant with others wishes and becoming overwhelmed with guilt and anxiety, we continue to say yes too often to what we don't want and no to what we truly crave.

I'll teach you why we commonly experience guilt and anxiety while building boundaries, and you'll learn how to release them on your own, for good. We're stopping this cycle, once and for all.

Last but not least, you'll gain more time to do what you love (even if that is taking a nap). Your people-pleasing days will be a thing of the past. Think about it: as you start to respect yourself, carve out certain people or situations from within your life, and set healthy boundaries, you'll quickly become the master of your schedule. Saying the word no to something or someone only allows you to say yes more authentically to something or someone that matters most to you. As you continue to say no, you'll get more comfortable with that little word and will begin to find yourself becoming less frustrated and less resentful.

More time on your hands for what you truly love to do with less resentment and frustration? Sign me up.

*Let's make more time
for the things you love.*

If you're curious about how the heck we're going to accomplish all of these major transformations, just stick with me; I plan to show you how. I designed this book based on my five-part system, the boundaries-with-soul method, and everything you'll need to begin to unlock your personal yes power can be found within these pages.

Even better, this book is designed specifically to help you along, step by step and chapter by chapter, with fill-in-the-blank questions, meditations, and blank journal pages just waiting for your thoughts.

BEFORE WE BEGIN

I want to assure you that most everyone you encounter is, in one way or another, going through this process as well, intentionally or not. Myself included. We are all in this together, so challenge yourself to remain patient, humble, and open to new ways of thinking throughout this process. As you read through this workbook, you may begin to notice involuntary shifts in your everyday life – this is all part of the progression of building boundaries. Trust the process, and keep an open mind and heart.

Givers have to set limits because takers rarely do.

| Irma Kurtz |

A Crash Course in Boundaries

Before we get serious about your boundaries, let's take a moment to learn just what I'm talking about when I say this word boundaries. There's some necessary groundwork we need to cover that will help you throughout this book, so grab a highlighter, and dial in; we're going to boundary school!

WHAT WE'RE NOT DOING

I'm going to keep this part short and straightforward—let's talk about what boundaries with soul aren't. Repeat after me:

- Boundaries with soul are not created in haste.
- Boundaries with soul are not built to isolate ourselves from the ones we love.

· Boundaries with soul are not an excuse to be rude or condescending.

· Boundaries with soul are not a hall pass to become high maintenance or excessively demanding.

· Boundaries with soul are not to be taken advantage of.

· Boundaries with soul are not an excuse to stay within our comfort zones.

· Boundaries with soul are not meant to make us boring.

WHAT WE ARE DOING

Using the authentic approach to building boundaries, we're going to build some boundaries with soul, ones that feel good to set. Even better, they will feel good to commit to for the long run.

THE BEGINNING

What exactly are boundaries? Plain and simple, boundaries are internal rules that directly govern which behaviors are okay with you and which behaviors are not. Why do we make these things so complicated? It's important to recognize that boundaries may vary widely between different people and situations and that these laws are unique to the person setting them. There's no right or wrong when it comes to boundaries, as long as they are reflective of that person's truest, most authentic self and honor that individual's personal values.

Boundaries are important because they give us a chance to define what is ours and what isn't ours. Creating clearly defined boundaries gently guides us to uncover just what in our lives is truly our responsibility and is worthy of our attention. When these limits exist, we allow ourselves to devote more time, effort, and energy to purposes that feel authentic to us and are important.

Also, when we become more defined about what is our responsibility, we also become a lot clearer on what isn't ours to worry about, to obsess over, or to prioritize. When this release of responsibility occurs, we are giving ourselves more opportunities to focus our time, attention, and love to what is ours and releasing the rest to the universe. Even better, when we value our personal boundaries, we then begin to honor the personal boundaries within those around us.

Boundaries with soul allow us to live from places of love.

THE KINDS OF BOUNDARIES

Within this idea of boundaries, I like to think there are two different types: boundaries we should respect within ourselves, or internal boundaries, and limits others need to comply with, or external boundaries.

Internal boundaries are quite simply rules within ourselves that we set for our personal behavior based off of what we value and what we deserve. Our internal boundaries most likely reflect our personal ethics and morals we hold to be true.

To help you out, here are some examples of strong internal boundaries:

· setting personal goals and committing to them, even when it's not easy

· honoring the limits we set around consuming food, drugs, or alcohol

· keeping our promises to others regarding our particular behaviors

On the contrary, external boundaries are rules around the behaviors and energy that we choose to accept, or not accept, from others. Think about the concept of external boundaries this way: Your body is your house, and the invisible energy that's always floating around you is your yard. Your external boundary is the fence that you build to protect your house and your yard from the people you don't want knocking on your door and asking for something from you or stealing your precious energy (and time!).

To help you out, here are some examples of strong external boundaries:

· telling others that their behavior is not okay with you

· putting your foot down when someone is asking too much from you

- speaking up at someone else's rude, condescending, or unsolicited remarks

In addition to internal and external boundaries, there's the idea of functional and relational boundaries. Keep in mind that either of these boundary types can possess either internal or external properties.

Quite simply, functional boundaries reveal your ability to adhere to a task, complete a goal, or perform a particular job. Functional boundaries have to do with integrity and discipline. Relational boundaries are associated with relationships and are centered on how well you can communicate with those with whom you are in a relationship, in some capacity or another. (Cloud and Townsend 2004[1])

THE SIGNS OF BOUNDARY VIOLATION

Typically, when individuals experience a boundary breach of some sort, their nervous systems immediately start to send signals throughout their bodies to alert them of this disruption. Becoming aware of this boundary breach is entirely up to us, as the one experiencing the violations, and get in touch with what's happening within our bodies.

A primal connection exists between our brain and our gut. We often talk about a "gut feeling" when we meet someone for the first time. We're told to "trust our gut instinct" when making a difficult decision or that it's "gut check time" when faced with a situation that tests our nerve and determination. This mind-gut connection is not just metaphorical. Our brain and gut are connected by an extensive network of neurons and a highway of chemicals and hormones that regularly provide feedback about how hungry we are, whether or not we're experiencing stress, or if we've ingested a disease-causing microbe. This information superhighway is called the brain-gut axis, and it provides constant updates on the state of affairs at your two ends. That sinking feeling in the pit of your stomach after looking at your post-holiday credit card bill is a vivid example of the brain-gut connection at work. You're stressed, and your gut knows it— immediately. (Sonnenburg and Sonnenburg 2015[2])

Have you ever heard of the fight-or-flight response? When the boundaries we are so delicately trying to build (or have already built) begin to be tested by another, our nervous systems immediately send our bodies into a state of fight or flight—a physiological reaction that occurs in response to a threat. During this reaction, we may begin to feel anxious or uneasy. Physically, we may experience tightening in our chests and sweaty palms and knots may take shape in our stomachs.

Pay attention when you start feeling these physical

symptoms, which are your body's way of communicating, because they're more than likely not occurring because you're dramatic or overreacting—your body is desperately trying to tell you something.

In addition to these physical symptoms of boundary disruption, we may begin to notice some emotional responses as well. Upon boundary intrusion, emotions of anger, frustration, and resentment may appear. Some immediately recognize these feelings and can take action right away to halt the progression of these emotions and the imminent boundary violation.

For others, these powerful emotions take a bit more time to simmer before bubbling to the surface. It may so happen that when they finally do show up, hours or days have passed, leaving the two incidences, boundary violation and experiencing strong emotions, seemingly unconnected and not at all related to each other. With practice, you will begin to draw associations between the two, and ultimately, will become faster at recognizing the trigger (or boundary violation) behind the specific emotions you're experiencing.

Unfortunately, if we ignore the symptoms of boundary violation and these emotional responses become the norm, and the excessive demands—placed by ourselves or others—continue to pile up, we may find ourselves in states of depletion, or emotional exhaustion.

Is anyone who is reading this burnt out?

Are you constantly forgetting the little things?

Maybe you're experiencing decision fatigue.

I'm talking about the moments in life when you're too exhausted to even begin to make a decision. For example, you're too tired to call the shots on what to make yourself or your family for dinner (not even caring whether it's healthy or not) because the major win for that day was just existing until dinnertime.

For others, when we're filled with unexpressed pent-up emotions from boundary violation, we find it difficult to make a decision. We come indecisive, and are unsure of what exactly we want because forgetting your own needs is quite easy to do when you're constantly living for others.

Those moments are exactly what I'm talking about when I mention experiencing emotional responses from continuous boundary violation.

Entering into the dangerous world of chronic emotional overextension tends to set us up for failure at some point in the future. After repeated letdowns and shortcomings, we may begin to wonder why we can't commit to our fabulous (and expensive!) gym memberships, adhere to the newest fad diets, or stick up for ourselves at work. We also begin to wonder why so many other people seemingly have it together while we just can't seem to get it right.

In the end, we often decide that the common denominator in these shortcomings is simply something wrong with us personally, usually having to do with being too (enter negative word here). Not once considering that maybe, just maybe, that's not the case. Give yourself a hug.

WHY DON'T WE JUST SET BOUNDARIES?

Here is where boundary cultivation work gets a bit hairy. Just as personal boundaries vary from person to person so too can the reasons boundaries are not set in the first place.

People often don't feel comfortable setting boundaries or saying no because these acts of rebellion may be perceived as selfish in today's society. Whether we are making holiday plans with family, politely declining to get even more involved in our children's schools, or finally telling our not-so-nice friends that we've had it with their negative attitudes, I can almost guarantee we will experience similar reactions from those on the other side of our boundary-building attempts.

Some of the reactions we might receive from others while setting our personal boundaries include, but are not limited to: frustration, confusion, push-back, subtle eye-rolling, and sometimes, complete support and understanding.

A lack of ability to build boundaries and say no goes deeper than being uncomfortable, and I whole-heartedly believe that our personal self-worth plays a significant role in our ability to say yes or no. When I polled a small group of women, overwhelmingly, the number one reason why they weren't setting boundaries was due to the fear of letting others down. I get that, and for a long time, I couldn't stand the feeling of knowing that I was intentionally disappointing another person.

Then one day, I wondered, why the hell are their feelings more important than my own?

Spoiler alert: they aren't.

Throughout this process of building boundaries with soul, you're going to let some people down. You must learn to be okay with that, as this acceptance is critical to your overall happiness.

To help you feel a bit more at peace with this whole letting-others-down scenario, here are some words of encouragement that I adore: "Brené Brown says in more than a decade of studying people; she found that those with the strongest boundaries were also the most compassionate. Individuals with a firm sense of what's okay and what's not set lines and stick to them. Guarding your personal boundaries doesn't make you cold-hearted and standoffish; it shows that you respect yourself, and in turn, you respect others." (Fry 2016[3])

In addition to the constant consideration of others' feelings, individuals working on building boundaries can frequently become so overcome with guilt and anxiety when faced with the opportunities to put their feet down that they back out at the last second and don't commit to the act. I have to tell you that this was me.

Until recently, I didn't connect the dots that my chronic stomachaches and sweaty palms had to do with boundary violation, and it took saying no to finally make me realize that my physical symptoms of stress were caused by a burning desire to stand up for myself.

For myself, I've discovered that my anxiety over building boundaries came out of the idea that something—a relationship, a job, a feeling—would crumble if I put my foot down, especially in the areas of my career and personal relationships. As you can guess, this way of living isn't sustainable, and it led to a lot of instances where I was walked all over and left with nothing but exhaustion, a lot of resentment, and some pints of my favorite ice cream. Consequently, I clung onto those around me even harder.

Do you see the vicious cycle that was created?

Looking back at that time, I honestly didn't think that I was worthy of saying no or requesting respect from certain individuals in my life. I convinced myself that everything would come tumbling down around me, and instead, I found myself living from a place of fear, scared to make a move or voice my desires. Simply tolerating a situation in life is not a way to live, at least not for me.

Little did I know that I had so much to gain from establishing boundaries that were constructed out of my deepest, truest values—my boundaries with soul.

Fairly quickly, the people and situations that no longer served me moved out of my life, and I found myself relieved to watch them go. Listen closely: In order to create a life you truly love, you must take the responsibility to make room for the right people, situations, and opportunities to enter your life.

BOUNDARY SHAMING

Instead of living wholeheartedly fulfilled and harmoniously balanced lives with soulful boundaries that serve our needs first, we are expected to give 110 percent, working ourselves to the bone just to prove our worth to our bosses, our companies, our families, or complete strangers. We aren't expected to stop and take care of our needs, much less think about them.

Side note: for many, their self-worth is only tied to their success within the workplace, completely disregarding any other signs of growth within their life, and that simply shouldn't be the case.

In the rare moments that we finally get enough courage to voice our needs for more boundaries (or breathing moments to ourselves), there's a high chance that our vocal ask will be met with pushback or criticism. Remember, if those around you don't respect their own personal boundaries, how the hell are they going to respect yours?

Wow, you must be selfish, huh?

I call this phenomenon of sticking up for what you want but being met with negative pushback from others boundary shaming. Personally, I've experienced boundary shaming while living in New York City quite a few times, but one of my boundary-shaming experiences stands out to me.

To set the stage, this story takes place during a transformational time for me. I had been doing the single-and-minglin' dance for almost a year, and an amazing man had just made himself a presence in my life. He'd actually been right under my nose the entire time, but that's a story for another time.

I was out to dinner with a few girlfriends and had decided not to drink for the week (what!) and quickly expressed that I wouldn't be partaking in the shared bottle of wine. After some odd remarks about how strange my soberness was, everyone got over it, and dinner was underway. I also mentioned to the group that I didn't feel like sharing everyone's meals, and that I would be ordering a meal for myself and only myself (whoa, you rebel!).

I literally could've cut the tension with a knife. As we finished up, the girls chatted about the idea of heading to a local trendy-casual bar for a few more drinks, which I politely declined. As a female, I'm no stranger to those subtle-but-not-so-subtle glances that say, "I can't believe you're not coming out with us. That's rude." I didn't want to head home because I wasn't drinking but because I was exhausted, and quite frankly, I wanted to get home to spend time with my boyfriend (he's now my fiancé) and my dog and unwind from the day.

As I climbed into a cab, I felt so guilty that I wasn't with my friends. I swore I could feel my friends talking about me and the fact that I had chosen to go home; their disappointed energy was still lingering around me. At the same time, I heard a small voice in my head that said, "Good for you! You stuck with your boundaries, and you're worthy of that. Get some rest, and spend time with the man you love. And guess what? You're not going to go to work hungover."

That tiny yet confident voice—pay attention to it.

MY WISH FOR YOU

My hope is that throughout these pages, you discover the possibilities that are waiting to be graciously ushered into your life. As you work through this book, I hope you find yourself with less anxiety and no guilt around sticking up for yourself and protecting your precious time and energy.

Even more so, I pray you find more time for the people that you love. Possibly, you'll find yourself digging into a new hobby or picking up an old one that used to bring you so much joy. My wish for you is that you learn how to say yes authentically and finally feel just how good that self-serving act feels.

And ultimately, I hope you realize that you're worth it. Loving yourself first and establishing boundaries within yourself and with others isn't selfish, and in the end, you'll be able to give that much more because you'll be putting up with that much less.

Are you ready? Let's dig in.

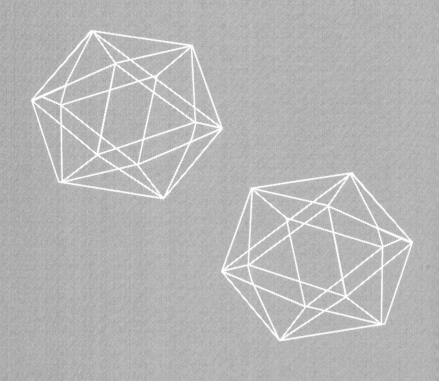

PART
Two

The authentic self
is the soul made
visible.

| Sarah Ban Breathnach |

STEP ONE
Find Your Authentic Self

Matt, a client of mine, came to me completely overwhelmed by his current way of eating. His sugar cravings, he said, ran his life. He felt he didn't know where to begin, and since Matt was forty-five and the father of two children, he wanted to get to the bottom of his food choices.

When we began his program, Matt adhered to the guidelines I set around his eating patterns—have no coffee after three o'clock in the afternoon, avoid pastries for breakfast, focus on healthy fats and protein, make friends with complex carbohydrates, add in vegetables at every meal—and we saw some real changes begin to take place. With some work, he felt less inflamed, and his skin showed it! His daily afternoon slump from hypoglycemic episodes began to fade away slowly.

That's not all of his progress though! Since Matt's career required him to work in the evenings, he was batch cooking for his family during the day and found himself enjoying the time he spent at the local market. Ever so slowly, his palette began to evolve, and he started to taste his food honestly; even the vegetables felt fresher and more vibrant. His sugar cravings went out the window.

Despite all of this success, Matt still felt like something in his life wasn't complete. After a few sessions of questioning and digging, we got to the bottom of it: he had stopped his morning chanting ritual.

He was a practicing Buddhist, but Matt had lost touch with what his spirituality meant to him and the value it added to his life. He got wrapped up in the idea that since he wasn't chanting and meditating to the imaginary standards made up in his mind, he just shouldn't do it at all. I gently encouraged him that practicing, no matter how "off" it may have been, was better than not practicing at all.

So, practice he did. Day by day, Matt began his morning meditation and chanting ritual, and he slowly found himself getting back in touch with his authentic self. He felt the light become a bit brighter and found himself yearning for more creative expression. Being a musician by trade, Matt decided that he was going to record new songs and perform them at a bar in Brooklyn because, why not?

Matt's authentic self yearned to live a more creative life, and through his recommitment to his daily spiritual practice (that's an internal boundary), he was able to realize just what he needed.

TAKE YOUR TURN

The first step in your journey to building healthy boundaries with soul is to get in touch with your authentic self. To start, let's talk about this idea of authentic self.

Together, these two words carry different meaning to different people, but to me, your authentic self is your truest being. This self is who you are at your core, and it embodies what you sincerely desire, what you value, and ultimately, who you are destined to be. It's your soul. It is perfectly in tune with the universe.

For me, when I'm truly in touch with my authentic self, it shows up in my body: I feel an overwhelming sense of calm, security, and balance. When I become disconnected from my authentic self, I get sweaty palms, and the familiar anxious knots begin to appear in my stomach. (I've given them the name Nauseated Knots.) When this happens, it's my cue to listen. I pay extra close attention, because chances are there's a boundary currently being violated within my space somehow.

FIND OUT WHAT YOU VALUE

To build boundaries with soul that you intend to keep around for a while, let's first figure out what you truly value:

· Is it your time?

· Is it your energy?

· Is it your emotional energy?

· Is it your family?

· Is it your home?

· Is it your health and wellness?

· Is it your integrity?

· Is it how you nourish yourself with the food you eat?

The list goes on, but all of these values have one thing in common: they're worth protecting.

We will be using two of my favorite tools to get a bit more in touch with your authentic, truest self: journaling and meditation. I invite you to use the space below and allow some of your values to make their way off the top of your head and onto the page. To help, think about what drives your daily behavior, or the voice that you hear inside your head when you're faced with a decision and the words or emotions you find popping up during your yoga practice, before you fall asleep, or when you're in the shower.

Here are a few of my chosen values:

· Humbleness

- Balance
- Honesty
- Playfulness
- Integrity
- Alignment with self
- Love

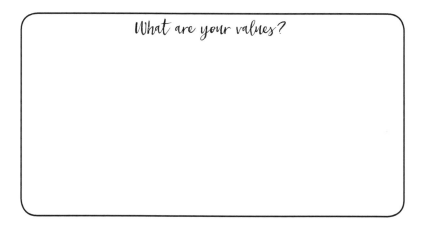

What are your values?

MEDITATION: FIND YOUR AUTHENTIC SELF

To take this practice of getting in touch with your authentic self a step further, please head to my website at CarleySchweet.com for a guided meditation titled "Finding Your Authentic Self."

This fifteen-minute meditation will allow for more clarity, insight, and mental release around what you value. Chances are you may discover something entirely new about yourself or get in touch with a lost past that has been dismissed and locked away.

When you're ready, please find a quiet space in a room you love, sit quietly with your hands palm-up on your knees, and listen along to the meditation video.

Welcome Back

Now, I want you to take a moment to write down the values you discovered about yourself during the meditation.

Now compare your two lists from premeditation and postmeditation that contain your values.

My postemeditation values

The values and emotions that are similar between the two lists, these are truly in line with your authentic self. They may be already visible in your daily life, or they might need a bit more practice. Remember these similar words. Highlight them, as these values are important to you.

The next step in this practice is to write these similar values on the list titled "My Authentic Desired Values." Go back to your postmeditation list, and look at the values that are different between pre- and postmeditation. Take a look at each value or emotion individually, and ask yourself why the value is there and whether it is a true value for you.

If the word is a true value for you, please add it to your authentic desired values list.

If it is not a true value for you, please cross it off your postmeditation list.

My authentic desire valuess

You may find that these lists are the same, and if so, that's great! You may find that you have to remove or add some new values, and that's totally fine.

After you've filled out your authentic desired values list, take note of whether you experienced any particular emotions or feelings during the practice. You may have felt calm, anger, tranquility, childlike playfulness, or anxiousness.

Finish These Statements

To build effective boundaries with soul, it's imperative that we begin to get in touch with what we're truly feeling. Questioning and journaling is a great tool to help us pause and reflect on the emotions we're experiencing or have recently experienced. Throughout this workbook, I will be asking you some simple, but thought-provoking, questions to help unlock some of what you're feeling and guide you on your boundary-building process.

Starting now.

Before the authentic desired values practice I felt:

During the authentic desired values practice, I felt:

After finishing the authentic desired values practice, I feel:

The final step for this chapter and to get in touch with your authentic self is to discover exactly who or what is holding you back from obtaining and upholding your values within your daily life.

Please keep in mind there are no right or wrong answers, and your writing is for you and you alone. Be gentle and graceful with yourself and your emotions, as you may experience some difficult feelings bubbling up during this practice. Note that there is no one to blame for living a life misaligned with your authentic values. Don't blame yourself, your partner, or your boss. This life is a learning experience, and building healthy boundaries where they're needed most will help to uphold your values and encourage you to live a life in alignment with your truest self.

Go ahead and take a moment to answer the question on the next page, in the spaces provided.

What are the three biggest changes that need to occur to live a daily life aligned with your core desired values?

Change #1

Change #2

Change #3

Wow, there's your starting point. Just within this first chapter, we've created your authentic desired values, and we've gotten more in touch with the three changes that need to occur to live lives aligned with those values. For those of you who have lost touch with what you desire and value within your lives, I hope you're feeling a bit more secure about who you are and what you stand for.

As you work through this book, please keep these values in mind. You may find yourself needing to refer back to them as we dive deeper into the remaining steps.

Examine
what you tolerate.
What you put up with,
you end up with.
What you allow,
continues.

| Karen Salmansohn |

STEP TWO
Feel for Your Boundaries

My parents got divorced when I was in high school. I was gearing up to leave for college in a nearby state, and they had waited to tell the news to my brother and me until I was close to graduating from high school.

The announcement of their divorce came as a big shock to us, but my brother and I are resilient people, and our parents were so supportive and loving that we got through it okay. I went off to college a few months later, and the whole situation seemed to become out of sight, out of mind. I always wondered when my parents' divorce would catch up to me, or if it ever would. In my opinion, I was constantly waiting for a shift in my personal relationships to occur—a lack of trust, narcissism, or pessimistic views of love—but it never happened.

The revelation that did occur was bigger than I ever could have predicted, and it challenged me to my core. In retrospect, the situation I'm about to describe to you has been a familiar one to me my entire life; I wasn't aware of just how familiar I'd been with this scenario until the all-too-common emotions that accompanied it were forced into my view.

I'm a feeler, a fixer, an empath. I'm almost too in touch with what I'm feeling and why. I was this way when I was younger, but I wasn't able to slow down, zoom out, and analyze situations as I can now. Instead, I bottled up how I was feeling and continued on my merry way, helping others, listening to their problems, and offering way too much advice while gaining little in return. I was internally anxious all the time and often found myself blowing up at my parents out of nowhere and crying myself to sleep at night for who knew what reasons.

My parents' divorce forced me to change that limiting behavior and, in turn, allowed me to truly uncover the boundary lines that already existed and were in dire need of reinforcement.

The tests of my limits that came along with my parents' split were nothing serious, but I knew if I let them continue, I would have to live with chronic Nauseated Knots and clammy hands. I would get phone calls, texts, and e-mails asking me to tell my mom something, to call my dad and have him call my mom, and to tell my dad to tell my brother to do something.

I totally obliged for a while, but as I became more aware of the fact that this messenger role was expected of me within my family, I knew I had to put an end to it. This process happened slowly, but with every situation that tested my limits, my noes became stronger and came out of my mouth with more oomph and less guilt.

Eventually, the messenger requests stopped coming altogether. I was finally free from my courier duties, and in turn, hopefully, my boundary lines encouraged everyone to communicate a bit better on their own, without involving me in the process.

TAKE YOUR TURN

Let's go a step further and begin to dig around for your personal boundary lines—I know they're there.

Throughout this chapter, our goal is to uncover the small pocket of space that exists where your comfort zone ends and the anxiety, anger, frustration, and resentment begin. By doing so, we are learning where to construct your soulful boundaries and finding out where these new limits will ultimately serve you best.

The overarching objective of this entire guide is to build boundaries that feel good to keep, and this chapter will help support that mission. Keeping your authentic value list in mind, I want to walk you through the practice that I call feeling around for your boundary lines. We will be digging around in the most honest and raw areas of your life for boundaries that might already exist, although they might be outside your conscious awareness. This practice is a critical step in forming real, authentic boundaries.

Additionally, this practice might reveal some patterns within your discoveries, and these insights are crucial for learning more about your triggers—what (and who!) presses your buttons. From there, you can begin to strategize the best way to build a healthy boundary between your triggers and yourself.

Some powerful patterns that tend to show up for most people are around relationships: food and the reasons we eat the way we do, friends and social commitments, family and expectations, lack of self-respect, work and its consistently extreme expectations or lack of balance, and so forth. By discovering a typical pattern, we can dig in just a bit deeper and get a clearer picture of not only what boundaries are needed but also where they need to occur.

The biggest reason I love this questioning practice is that it can evoke some strong emotions, so please allow yourself to be vulnerable, and know that there are no right or wrong answers. To get the most out of this exercise, let the answers flow out of you. Don't leave any thought unwritten. The moment a particular word, situation, person, or emotion comes to mind, write it down. Think about using this practice as a way to enter an almost meditative state, where you can get closer to your truest desires, worries, fears, and vulnerable spots.

Before we begin, I recommend that you get comfortable (if you're not already) and give yourself some time to think each sentence through. For me, it helps to repeat each sentence fragment out loud, followed by each of the answers that come to mind. If you're feeling up to it, I challenge you to come up with ten answers for each. The deeper you dig, the more you'll uncover, and the closer you'll return to balance.

People are not allowed to ...

Take a breath.

I have a right to ...

Breathe.

To protect my time and energy, I'm allowed to ...

Exhale.

Thanks for being so honest here. I know sometime these questions can cause some new emotions to bubble up, but those emotions are just what we are seeking. Keep in mind, that the feelings you're experiencing in this exact moment could be similar to the emotional and physical symptoms you may have been ignoring during times of personal boundary violation. Only now, you may be a bit more aware of what you're feeling and why you're feeling it, allowing yourself to become more in touch with what's happening in the present moment.

Thank yourself for allowing yourself to feel these emotions right now, your boundaries will thank you later.

Everything I need
is already within me.

| Louise Hay |

STEP THREE
Grow Your Self-Worth

Steve is a client of mine that touched my soul. He worked in corporate America, but decided that he wanted to start his own business and quit working for the man. After a few months of hard work, he did just that. He envisioned a flexible schedule, more vacations, and time to work out in the mornings. Quickly, his business began to boom, and his work-life balance became virtually nonexistent.

Something needed to change, fast.

When I first started working with Steve, he was waking up at five-thirty in the morning to start answering client e-mails, then he rushed off to appointment after appointment during the day. At night, he spent his hours writing proposals for potential customers he had seen just a few hours before. There was not a moment to himself in sight.

When he finally collapsed into bed at eleven, he found himself waking up in the middle of the night, checking the time on his phone, and getting sucked into vortices of client e-mails that had come through in the wee hours of the morning. Then the anxiety would set in. Reading those client e-mails when he should've been sleeping caused extreme anxiety and wouldn't allow him to fall back to sleep, leaving him exhausted for his early wake-up the following morning. The cycle continued until Steve decided that he had enough respect for himself (and his business) and put an end to his runaround once and for all.

See, Steve was living from a scarcity mind-set, and he was always worried that he wasn't good enough and that every client who turned him down was a mark against his self-esteem. The middle-of-the-night worrying and the constant need to please was coming from a place of lack—a fear of being turned down. If you do everything the way you're supposed to, no one will be able to say no to you, right? Wrong.

On a side note, when you're living with a scarcity mind-set, you are under the belief that there is never enough—food, money, time, love, support, and so on. In turn, every word spoken or emotion felt stems from a place of lack and worry. You may become obsessed with what it is you need instead of focusing on what you already have or the opportunities that already surround you.

Together, Steve and I worked on shifting his mindset from one of fear and shortage to one of opportunity and abundance, and it took reevaluating his self-worth and self-respect to get there. You may ask what this has to do with boundaries.

Well, one afternoon, when Steve had been dealing with a particularly difficult potential client, something clicked. Instead of bending over backward to send the perfect proposal to her, he decided not to move forward and politely declined $20,000 worth of work because his sanity was more important than his clients' temporary discomfort.

Wow, talk about a boundary!

When Steve put his foot down and said no to someone that wasn't serving his best needs, he was able to open himself up to new opportunities, both with his time and his energy. Do you remember what I said before? To life a life you love, you must make room for the right people, situations, and opportunities to enter your life.

Steve saved hours of work by not writing a proposal for that client and was able to shift his focus to other tasks that felt good to accomplish. By shifting his mind-set from scarcity to abundance, he cultivated more feelings of self-respect. And honestly, he told me it felt damn good to finally tell someone no. I believe it.

WHAT YOU'LL BE DOING

Throughout this third step, we are going to work on growing your self-worth, just as Steve did for himself and his company. I'm going to challenge you to shift your mindset from putting others first to putting yourself first, and in turn, your self-respect will begin to flourish.

You're going to hear me say this over and over again: it's not rude to put yourself first. One of my biggest pet peeves is when someone pays another person a compliment by saying, "She always puts others first; she's the nicest person I know." Yeah, that person may be helpful and caring, but have you ever stopped and asked that chronic put-others-first person how he or she is actually feeling? Chances are, those people might be harboring a lot of resentment, frustration, anger, anxiety, and maybe even some feelings of guilt. Additionally, they may feel like they're missing out on certain aspects of their life, or living a life unfulfilled, due to the fact they're constantly worried about pleasing everyone around them, without ever taking a moment to themselves.

As we work through this chapter, please keep in mind that all of our needs are different when it comes to internalizing our self-respect. There is one thing I believe we all have in common: what we need most to live balanced and fulfilled lives already exists within us; we just need to un-lock it and respect it. When we learn to respect ourselves, we are blessed with the opportunity to teach others to comply with us, our boundaries, and our desires.

Without the proper self-respect, it's easy to overlook the value in the boundaries we are attempting to build, and we may find ourselves writing off our boundaries as not worth the effort. In reality, they're completely worth it.

When it comes to asking others to respect our boundar-ies, we may feel selfish for asking because deep down, we may not feel worthy of asking others to recognize our per-sonal limits. At this moment when feelings of selfishness creep up, we need to dig a bit deeper, examine why we feel unworthy, and release those fears to the universe because they simply aren't true.

Another scenario we may find ourselves in is when we're presented with the opportunity to say no, we may feel compelled to agree to a situation that doesn't sit right with our authentic selves, purely because we feel like we have to. Later on, as the commitment approaches, we end up regretting our decision and backing out at the last minute, often coming up with a lame excuse as to why we can't fol-low through on our promise.

Wouldn't it just be easier to say no in the first place?

A DECLARATION OF SELF-RESPECT

You are worthy of living a life in alignment with your authentic desired values, and you're born with the right to accept or reject people, situations, or energies that do not align with your authentic desired values. In case you need a reminder, you're worthy of doing the following things:

Exercising your right to say no

Having the words you speak heard as the truth

Receiving honest feedback

Giving and accepting pure and unconditional love

Taking a vacation away from technology

Being respected by all those you meet

Getting a good night's sleep

Having the power to change your mind

Listening to your intuition

Having the choice to leave those who don't serve you

Experiencing complete acceptance from everyone
you meet (and yourself)

Accessing healthy food and making empowered
decisions around eating

Saying yes wholeheartedly

_____

_____

_____

I've also included three blank spots in the list as an opportunity to add in your own worthiness declarations, just like I did for you. Since we've gotten you a bit more in touch with your authentic desired values, these blanks might be a bit easier to fill in than they were before we got started on your boundary-building journey.

What is your next challenge?

- Accept these worthiness declarations as true.
- Repeat them to yourself.
- Write them down.
- Post them on your mirror.
- Soak up the ones that feel good, right in this moment.
- Review these every day.

Now that we've become a bit more comfortable knowing about and believing in what we're worthy of, let's do some digging around to uncover a bit more about ourselves—this is an exciting space to play around in, isn't it? To tap into what's holding you back from believing these worthiness declarations are true or from making these statements your reality, spend some time answering the three questions on the next page.

QUESTIONS TO ANSWER

What do I need to do to regain my personal power?

Now that you've pinned down some action items to take to help restore your power and shift out of a fear-based mentality, it's time to chat about personal needs. Ideally, your boundaries that we are creating are not only built off of your authentic values but are also based on your human needs: to exist, to thrive, to give, to love, to empathize, to dream, and to hope.

What personal needs currently feel most neglected?

You're doing a great job. Identifying which individual needs demand the most assistance is a major step in cultivating some lasting self-respect. Now, it's time to look even further inward and ask yourself what you've been doing to disrespect yourself. Let's uncover some ways to reverse those habits.

Doesn't it feel good to take a moment to think about how you can treat yourself just a bit better? The second

How can I better respect myself, my power, and my needs?

that you decide you're worth treating well is the moment you begin to teach others to do the same.

Frequently, when it comes to building healthy boundaries (and sticking to them), we feel powerless when attempting to move forward. To me, this feeling occurs because we find ourselves trapped in a place between what we think we should do, what we want to do, and what others think we should do. That space of powerlessness and fear is a scary place to exist, as the scarcity mindset, narcissism, and negativity all thrive in this environment, often stripping us of our personal power to say yes to building healthy boundaries.

If you're feeling a bit overwhelmed from this chapter's work, please know that those feelings are completely normal and expected. Sifting through the places and spaces that we're neglected and lacking respect can be difficult, but I can almost guarantee you it's worth it.

In order to grow our self-esteem, it's important to first figure out where we're lacking, where we can grow, and where we can encourage more respect and personal power.

A NOTE ON SELF-CARE

Growing your self-esteem and personal self-worth is not easy work. This process takes time, trial and error, and a lot of forgiveness, but I can certainly promise you that this practice is worth it.

When I first started out on my journey to increase my self-esteem and self-worth, the gym was instrumental for me. For an hour a day, I was committing to no one but myself. I wasn't worried about who was texting me or what e-mails I missed. I wasn't worried about what was going on at the office. I wasn't concerned with anything but myself. I didn't realize it at the time, but those hours I poured myself into the gym were a major form of self-care.

Working out is still an important part of my self-care routine, but my rituals around taking care of and loving myself have morphed into something smaller and more manageable. They're habits that I can jump into first thing in the morning and spend five to ten minutes doing before bed:

· They're not groundbreaking or going to save the world;

· They're not high tech or expensive;

· They're mine, and when I commit to them, I feel good;, and that's enough for me.

Are you curious about how I show myself some self-love?

· By making the bed every morning so I have a warm and clean place to crawl into at night

· By taking an invigorating hot shower laced with my favorite essential oils like eucalyptus or peppermint

· By making a flavored water (I love cucumber mint!)

· By indulging in a hot detox bath, complete with Epsom salts, a mud mask, and sleepy tea

· By putting body butter on my feet and then layering on lavender essential oil, followed by some cozy socks

· By diffusing a sleepy bedtime blend of essential oils as I wind down for the evening

· By having a regimented skin-care routine that includes luxurious-feeling lotions and oils

When you take a moment, no matter how small, to honor yourself in some way, your self-esteem grows. Something inside clicks and says, "I'm worth taking this detox bath, so I must be worth other good things too." You instantly open yourself up to other pockets of self-care and invite all the love into your space.

The ego is the false
self—born out of fear
and defensiveness.

| John Donahue |

STEP FOUR
Recognize and Abandon Fear

My former client Sarah had a sad past with her ex-boyfriend. She gave him everything, and how did he repay her? He cheated on her more than once. Being the loving person that she is, Sarah repeatedly took him back, telling herself that his infidelity was a problem on her end and that she was lacking something, causing her boyfriend to stray.

Throughout this rocky relationship, Sarah continually violated her personal boundaries by allowing his disrespectful behavior to have a place in their commitment to each other. Sarah was too afraid to stick up for herself and defend her oh-so-delicately built boundaries out of fear of being left.

Wait, wasn't the boyfriend the one doing the cheating?

Eventually, Sarah and her ex-boyfriend broke off their relationship, although they continued to talk, and she continued to beat herself up for not being what she thought he wanted. Over the next few months after the breakup, Sarah and her ex continued to communicate via e-mail and text, and one day, they took it as far as—well, you know what—one last time.

See, the problem with that one last dance was that Sarah's ex already had a new significant other in his life, but Sarah was convinced this act of love was going to win him back.

She was wrong.

Sarah and her ex finally parted ways for good, and Sarah found herself alone and pissed off. Her ex was now happily married and had a baby on the way, and where was she? Let's just say that she wasn't where she wanted to be.

After a few more months of unselfishly focusing on herself and committing her days to healing, Sarah finally saw the light. She realized that throughout the course of her relationship, her fear of asking for what she wanted, both physically and emotionally, had caused to her violate and abandon her personal boundaries altogether. In turn, she allowed her ex's disrespectful behavior to continue, and she beat herself up in the process.

Sarah is now doing wonderfully on her own and has gotten in touch with her truest self in the process. Her fear of asking for what she requires in her personal relationships is slowly fading. She's learning to let go of her pent-up frustration and resentment and is beginning to live her life leaning more toward love. She understands that she did not cause her boyfriend's unfaithfulness, and she is not to blame.

WHAT YOU'LL BE DOING

Learning to recognize fear is a crucial step in learning how to build healthy boundaries with soul. As we're going about in our daily lives, there are probably multiple instances when we're faced with decisions about whether to adhere to our boundaries or give in to them. More often than not, in the early stages of forming boundaries, it's easiest to give into the fear and allow our days to continue, even though deep down, we know this isn't the right path for us. When we give in to decisions, it's possible we are only letting our egos win and are completely disregarding our higher selves.

The reason that some of us have such a difficult time feeling secure about asking for boundaries boils down to the internal conflict between our egos and our higher selves. Instead of leaning into love, most of us tend to lean into fear and quickly become overwhelmed with feelings of anxiety, guilt, and frustration. Maybe those emotions don't show up right away, but they certainly will someday—just ask Sarah.

TAPPING INTO THE EGO AND HIGHER SELF

Within ourselves, two conscious voices exist: the ego and the higher self. I believe that two voices will always exist, but it is our responsibility to train and strengthen our minds to seek the voice of the higher self and gently guide our responses to follow our intuition, our purest intentions. You're already a bit more in touch with your intuition and higher self just by completing step one of this workbook: getting in touch with your authentic self.

WHAT THE EGO IS

The ego's primary job is survival. This inner part of ourselves has been conditioned year after year to protect us and serve us, but ultimately, it ends up becoming rooted in fear and drawing future values based on past situations that may or may not be accurate. This voice thrives on our anxiety and fear, and often, we can find ourselves lost in downward spirals of stress and fear that shouldn't even exist in the first place. We become convinced that every problem we have in our lives is because we are not enough, and we find ourselves not doing anything about it because we are genuinely convinced we are not worthy.

Thanks, Ego.

When it comes to what the ego desires, the ego is not content with what we already have around and within us.

68

Remember Steve? His ego was forcing him to live with a scarcity mind-set, one that convinced him that what he currently had in terms of clients and finances was not enough; this, in turn, caused Steve to live a life of anxiety around the looming feeling of always being broke. As we learned, those feelings were not reality, and Steve shifted his mind-set from egoist scarcity to one of abundance.

The power of the ego is so authoritative that it can come across our minds as the only option, possibly overriding the other conscious voice that exists within our bodies. Because we are individuals that constantly want to do the right thing, it's very easy to fall into the ego's persuasive trap, as we find ourselves doubting the tiny voice within that is attempting to guide us in the opposite direction.

Take a moment now to think of someone that leaves you feeling emotionally and physically exhausted after you leave their presence. What is it about that person that drains you? For me, I find it emotionally taxing to be in same space of consistently negative individuals. The type of men and women that can't seem to find anything positive to say, no matter what situation is placed in front of them. In the past, these individuals would wear me down and stress me out, as I took it upon myself to attempt to change the way they viewed the world.

That doesn't work.

If one's thoughts and behaviors are being mostly controlled by their ego, their outward behavior (and internal thoughts) reflects that mentality, and if you're a naturally intuitive person that has a good dialogue with your own ego, it's usually pretty easy to pick up on as an outsider.

THE SEVEN CHIEF FEATURES

As humans, we have our personality traits and, according to the Michael Teachings, we also have our chief features. Unlike a personality trait that is inherently neutral, a chief feature is dominant negative attitude that seems to be part of your nature, and can quickly become a destructive pattern of thinking, feeling, and acting. Those that struggle with their chief feature may oftentimes find themselves stumbling through the parts of their lives affected by this block, as it can be quite convincing.

Our chief feature is directly associated with our ego. This feature started to shape in our early childhood, and has slowly made its way into every aspect of our lives. Every single person has this stumbling block, but some have done enough personal growth work and reflection to not only recognize our chief feature, but deal with it effectively.

These features, or character flaws, are based off the Michael Teachings, and are listed from the most introverted to the most extroverted.

The Seven Chief Features

1. Self-Deprecation—belittling/undervaluing oneself

2. Self-Destruction—sabotaging/punishing/harming oneself

3. Martyrdom—denying responsibility for oneself

4. Stubbornness—resisting change in one's life

5. Greed—selfish over indulgence, over compensation

6. Arrogance—inflating, exalting, overvaluing oneself

7. Impatience—intolerance of frustration/objection/delay

As we are all human, we possess all seven of these chief features on some level, possibly even our behavior has been influenced by one of the characteristics at one point or another. Chances are, as you read through this list, there was one in particular that stuck out to you, one that struck a chord, or maybe gave you that unsettling feeling in the pit of your stomach.

The good news? These character flaws can all be overcome, as we become more conscious and aware of our feelings, our reactions, our triggers, and why we feel the way we do. When this happens, our chief feature becomes a catalyst for positive change within our lives. If we continue to live our lives on the path we're currently on, we may begin to develop a lasting, deep-engrained character flaw, one that certainly does not serve us.

OUR HIGHER SELVES

I find that the best way to describe the higher self is to think about a time that you experienced a gut reaction. Possibly, there was a time you felt a gentle nagging or a slight uneasiness in your stomach when faced with a given situation. Similar to how the fight-or-flight response communicates to the body the need for immediate action, the higher self has its own way of sharing a need for a response; we just need to listen to the subtle cues that are being sent to our bodies.

The phrase listen to your gut is around for a reason, right?

This feeling of a gut reaction is, in fact, your intuition, or your higher self. The conscious voice of the higher self is soft and gentle, but when its presence is acknowledged, a warm feeling of knowledge and empowerment gently arises within the body. I like to believe that it is buzzing with abundance and does not consider fear or anxiety as an option when making decisions. The higher self ultimately knows what's best; all we have to do is listen carefully.

As I mentioned earlier, when I set boundaries that are faithful to my values and encompass what I feel to be right in my soul, I feel balanced, grounded, and complete. For a fleeting moment, I feel a gentle warmth come over my body and soul. In this second of recognition, I know I'm making the right choice, even if it's a huge life decision, such as deciding to move in with my boyfriend after three months of dating or quitting my corporate job to embark on work more aligned with my soul (like writing this book!).

Now, take a moment and think of someone in your life that you love to spend time with. This person could be a loved one, a mentor, a teacher, or maybe even someone you met on the street. When you are with this person, you feel happy, light-hearted, and full of love and joy. Your relationship with each other is almost effortless, and it's as if their energetic frequencies directly match yours, leaving you feeling fully charged and bursting at the seams with good vibes. You are already looking forward to the next time you see them.

That feeling? That's what I feel when I'm in touch with and honoring my higher self.

Your Turn

Take a deep breath. Feel what's going on inside of you right at this exact moment.

Ultimately, the best advice I can give to help you move closer to your higher self is to listen honestly to your gut. When you find yourself in a situation that presents the opportunity for a decision to be made, pay attention to what you're feeling, both physically and mentally. Don't discount the subtleties. Those are what we're searching to discover.

For now, it's necessary to dig a bit deeper into how you feel and react in certain situations. From there, we will walk through a few questions to help dissect what you've discovered.

Finish These Statements

I feel myself becoming most negative when:

I struggle finding patience with:

Something I worry about is:

The outcome of this situation is in my control. __ Yes __ No

If no, I am willing to let this worry go? __ Yes ___No

I am good at:

It feels good to:

I am grateful for:

I pride myself on being:

When having conversations with others, I get anxious when:

Questions to Answer

What patterns exist within your responses?

What are you currently worried about
that isn't in your control?

What positive personal characteristics and qualities do
you possess that are being ignored or forgotten?

Hopefully, this exercise gives a little bit more insight as to where your ego is ruling and your higher self is hiding (or shining!).

The times when we are leaning toward fear and worry about not being, doing, or having enough, we are listening to our egos. When we feel our patience tested, driving us to believe that situations must turn out in certain ways on our terms, our egos are in control.

Alternatively, the higher self tends to seek the good in us. The higher self is not boastful or bragging; it simply is. The times when we lean toward seeing all situations and people through a lens of love and choose to accept them for what they truly are, when we embrace all that we are, all that we will be, and live closer to the light, we are living lives in more alignment with our higher selves.

THE BEAUTY OF HARMONY

In addition to differentiating between the two voices of the ego and higher self, it's important to keep in mind the beautiful idea of harmony. Harmony is the art of mastering your emotions when responding to situations—a complete integration of the ego and the higher self. When we are in harmony, we do not allow our knee-jerk emotions and reactions to define or control us, especially in the act of setting boundaries with soul.

To keep our internal balance flowing, in times that test our strength or our worth, it's imperative to remember not to give in to the ego and the emotions that come with it. We cannot let our responses turn into reactions, as this way of communicating with ourselves and others is not in line with living in congruity with our higher selves.

When in new or stressful situations, practice responding instead of reacting.

Follow your higher self.

WHEN (AND WHY) THE EGO SHOWS UP

The ego will inevitably show up, especially when you're flexing your newly discovered boundary muscles. When the anger hits or the anxiety begins as you start to vocalize your need for boundaries, I urge you to look around and see who is doing the talking—are you hearing your ego or your higher self?

For me, my palms used to get sweaty just thinking about the idea of telling people what I needed, purely out of fear of letting them down or giving them a reason to walk away. Yikes! Those instances were just my ego doing the communication, driving my behavior and, ultimately, leaving me full of resentment and frustration.

Let me explain my ego in action.

I lived with two very close friends right after college for

almost three years. I seriously couldn't have survived New York City without them—the late-night bar sessions, the early-afternoon bagel runs, the countless hours curled up on the couch laughing and gossiping, and the never-ending emotional and moral support.

Then, things got pretty serious with my boyfriend, and the two of us decided to move in together into an apartment of our own. In the New York City apartment life, the start and end dates of leases rarely match up perfectly, leaving you with either a few months of paying double rent or a few months of needing someone to sublet your room from you.

I needed the latter.

I also needed to have a talk with both of my roommates, and I wanted to do it privately, just one-on-one, to give each of us time to chat individually about how my upcoming move would affect their lives, the apartment structure, finances, and so forth. As you can only imagine, my stomach was in knots from the first day Corbin and I discussed moving in together, when in reality, I should have been over-the-moon excited. I mean, of course, I was! I just couldn't shake the anxious feeling about what (and how) I would tell my roommates.

Here are some of the initial thoughts that swirled around in my brain:

- "Don't you feel so mean leaving them with an open room so you can go live with your boyfriend?"
- "Isn't it super disrespectful of you to do that to those girls—they've had your back since day one, so can't you just hang around for another year?"
- "Wow, how can you be so irresponsible? You've only been dating this guy three months."
- "Are you sure you're ready for this?"
- "I mean, how are you going to afford this move?"
- "What if it doesn't work out? Won't you be embarrassed?"

I fretted over telling my roommates for almost two weeks. I called my mom every single day to have her walk me through the steps, I wouldn't stop talking to Corbin about it, and I was sick to my stomach when the opportunity to bring up the conversation approached.

And then I did it.

It sucked at first, and I felt so incredibly awkward, but then, I was beyond relieved. I felt at peace, calm, and so excited to build a new future with the man I loved. I'm so glad that I didn't let my ego stop me.

In retrospect, my ego was my biggest critic throughout those two weeks. I almost convinced myself that I couldn't go through with telling my friends the truth about my move, and I constantly thought of excuses to delay the conversation. I almost believed the stories I told myself that I was a heartless, cold bitch because I wanted to start the next chapter of my life; I mean, how cruel is it to treat yourself that way?

That's my ego. She's stubborn and self-deprecating. She's also no longer the boss of me.

The ego loves to show up in the moments we feel challenged—starting a new company, quitting an old job, moving across the country, moving in with a new significant other, or embarking on a new relationship—and when our vulnerability is at its highest.

The ego tells us that we are not smart enough to run our companies, not well-enough liked to make new friends in a new city, or not worthy enough to be in a respectful partnership. Most likely, none of those are true. As I mentioned before, the voice of the ego is a powerful one and can be very, very persuasive at first, and if putting ourselves out into the world and building healthy boundaries isn't a vulnerable situation, then I don't know what is.

ABANDONING FEAR

If you're finding yourself nodding vigorously at the idea of an overactive ego and some seriously strong chief features, don't fret. Personally, I think the situations when the ego shows up are great learning opportunities, but we must be in tune with what we're experiencing in that moment to fully understand what the ego is trying to communicate.

It is in our darkest moments that we often find our light.

By using these darker moments as chances to slow down, breathe, and acknowledge what we're feeling, we set ourselves up to get even more in touch with our higher selves and move that much closer to saying no more often and saying yes authentically. It is in these moments that we must learn to abandon our egos and our fears and get more in touch with our higher selves. It is here that we must learn to trust ourselves and remember we are worthy.

In these fragile moments, we must learn to lean in to the discomfort of the situation and look for the light. We must trust ourselves enough to abandon our fears and to believe that our higher selves will safely guide us to where we're supposed to be.

To help leave fear behind and trust the process that's unfolding, I use affirmations. I make them my phone background, pin them on Pinterest, and silently repeat them to myself as needed. Here are a few of my favorite affirmations that you can repeat after me:

· I do not have to be nice to those who are not kind to me.

· I have a right to say no without explaining myself.

· I can choose what I share with others, and no one can take that from me.

- I have the right to live in harmony with my higher self.

- I'm not perfect, and that's okay.

- I am completely acceptable, just the way I am, in this exact moment.

MEDITATION: TUNING IN TO HIGHER SELF

To get in touch with your higher self just a bit more, please head to my website at CarleySchweet.com for a guided meditation titled "Tuning in to Your Higher Self."

This meditation will allow for more clarity around what your higher self desires and values. Chances are, you may discover something entirely new about yourself, and hopefully, you'll get in a bit more touch with what the voice of your higher self is trying to communicate.

When you're ready, please find a quiet space in a room you love, sit quietly, and listen along.

Welcome Back

As you may have noticed, tuning into your higher self is very emotional work. As you listened to the meditation, it's quite possible there were certain sentences that stuck out to you but you're unsure why.

Hear me out.

The lines that resonate are the pieces of ourselves that we must work on in order to move forward and get in touch with our higher self. Something about those words resonated within you, and it's possible the gentle attraction you felt was truly a call to action. A call to create growth in your life and a call to connect to yourself a bit deeper.

Take a moment below and highlight the statements from the meditation that you felt a pull towards. Remember these as you move forward in strengthening your relationship with your higher self.

I am ebbing and flowing, but grounded and secure.

I am constantly growing, but I am not changing who I am. I am slowly becoming more and more me and discovering parts of me that were previously hidden.

I am becoming aware that what I admire about other people is already in me, I just need to access it.

I am also realizing that what I don't care for in other people is already in me. I will not judge myself for this, rather accept this truth and use it to grow.

Realizing that I can do whatever I want to do—that when I'm authentic and true to myself, the universe will provide me with what's truly meant to be.

That fear is a sign that I'm on the right path. I understand the importance of not feeding this fear, rather accepting that bliss is nearby, I just have to keep moving forward.

Not to apologize for who I was, who I am, or who I am going to be.

You have to decide
what your highest
priorities are and have
the courage—
pleasantly, smilingly,
nonapologetically—
to say "no"
to other things.
And the way to do
that is by having
a bigger "yes"
burning inside.

| Stephen Covey |

STEP FIVE
Say Yes Authentically

I loved my corporate fashion job; I really did. My coworkers were inspiring and amazing, the clothes were incredible, and there was always something exciting coming down the pipeline. I worked my butt off, day in and day out, constantly hoping that deep burning desire to serve others and make a lasting impact would someday be fulfilled—but it wasn't.

My purpose started to take place about three and a half years into my corporate life, and it took someone asking what I wanted to be doing in five years to make me realize that the work I was doing and what I was working toward weren't actually what I wanted to be pursuing at all.

On a side note for those wondering, yes, I got my undergraduate degree for something completely different than the work I do now—apparel merchandising and business, to be exact. Bottom line: don't let the work and education you've already invested in derail you from following your authentic yes.

I took my thinking back to square one; I knew I had to make a change.

Staying in on a Saturday night, I began researching holistic careers, personal training, and nutrition work; anything that sparked my yes burning inside. Once I found my path, I knew. It felt like everything I had been practicing, doing, and dreaming about all aligned into one purpose: I wanted to become a holistic coach. I wanted to help others live lives of balance and to help them realize that food is not meant to be restricted but loved. In short, to help others like myself.

Almost instantly after committing to going back to school, I felt a sense of relief, and a gentle warmth swept over my body. I knew that I had made the right choice, and I didn't care what it took to make this career switch work; I was determined.

I had found my authentic yes, and I could feel it with every single fiber of my being. That single moment felt like it was the exact place I was meant to be at that point in my life, and it felt damn good. Of course, it was slightly terrifying, but I believed that bliss was on the other side of fear.

THE TIME TO BEGIN

You're here at the final step. Take a deep breath in, and then let it out.

I must admit, the area you'll find yourself in—between abandoning your fear around saying no and learning how to say yes authentically—can be an emotionally trying one. Learning to say yes authentically is the point in the process when the ego likes to pop in and challenge your yes-saying power. I have hopes that since you're now so much more aware of how the ego manifests itself, you're finding letting go of these emotions around saying no a bit easier.

Just like getting comfortable with the idea of building healthy boundaries, learning to say yes authentically to the people and opportunities you want to have in your life takes some practice. The good news is, you've done a lot of the foundational dirty work already as you've worked through this book. Getting in touch with your authentic self and creating your authentically desired values, feeling around for your boundary lines to get a bit more in touch with where you stand emotionally, growing your personal self-respect, and poking holes in the areas in your life you deserve just a bit more respect and support—these all lead to a place of authentic yesses.

These learnings are fundamental as you move forward with this last step of learning to say yes authentically.

WHEN TO SAY YES

Think back, and remember the emotions and feelings that bubbled up when thinking about your noes—anxiety, frustration, and anger—and recall how they made you feel. These emotions certainly didn't want to make you agree to something, and in reality, they made you want to turn the other way and shut the door behind you. Since you weren't in touch with your boundary-building power quite yet, you might have said yes to those situations anyway.

Learning how and when to say yes is the same process as discovering your boundary lines and your voicing your noes, just with a different set of emotions. The glorious yes burning inside of you becomes clearer with every opportunity or situation you encounter, and from there, the new yes feelings of excitement, genuine interest, opportunity, and pure joy begin to grow.

I challenge you: the next time you find yourself faced with an opportunity of any kind, give your mind a few moments to get in touch with how you feel. A quick body scan will most likely give you a few clues as to what's going on. Keep your mind receptive to the yes responses—a peaceful, overwhelming calm; a warm feeling of love; a pull to somehow get closer; a small smile; or a slight nervousness, but the confidence to know you can do it. These feelings and intuitions are your higher self assuring you that the opportunity in front of you deserves an authentic yes.

THE FINAL QUESTION

The beauty in the art of building boundaries and learning to say no is that you become equipped with an ability to say yes, full of excitement, love, hidden opportunity, and a chance to challenge yourself. Chances are, most of your old yesses were filled with resentment, frustration, and lack of enthusiasm, and they were honestly downright irritating to follow through with when all was said and done.

> *How do I want to feel when saying yes to something?*

Hopefully, after some practice, you'll begin to feel the difference between those two different types of yesses.

NOW'S THE TIME

Now is the time for you to say yes authentically but also to say no. And now is the time to have that little two-letter word respected by all parties in your life—your mom, your sister, your dad, your best friend, your significant other, your blind date, your boss, and most importantly, yourself.

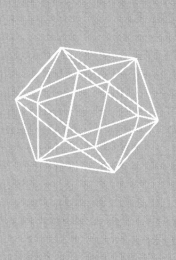

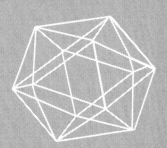

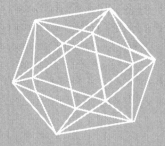

PART Three

Learn to say no with love. Learn to say yes and truly mean it. Build your boundaries with soul.

| Carley Schweet |

Some Parting Words

As you move forward with the new mind-set of exercising your no and living your authentic yes, please keep in mind a few things:

- We cannot change the actions of others; we can only control how clearly we set and communicate our soulful boundaries.

- We may have to physically demonstrate our boundaries—sometimes, communication won't be enough. You can do this simply through your body language; for example, not hugging a stranger when a handshake is sufficient, taking a step back while engaged in a conversation, or wearing clothing that protects your personal energy, such as a long cardigan or scarf to bundle yourself up in.

- There will be people who test your boundaries, and these people may be very close to you, like a partner or a family member. Stick to your guns about when to draw the line, and don't be afraid of temporarily upsetting someone—if they have nothing but love for you, they'll understand.

- Some people will have a hard time understanding your new boundaries. This does not mean they don't care for you or that you need to cut them out of your life. By communicating your reasons behind your newly established boundaries, you may help the affected parties see that this barrier formation is simply not about them, and it's purely for your ultimate personal happiness.

- You need to back up your boundaries with love. Assure others that your new no is not coming from a bad place, and do not withdraw your love from the relationship or situation. Explain to others that you're practicing loving yourself first in order to love others more fully.

- The ways others respond to your boundaries are not your responsibility. What is your responsibility is how you respond to others, especially if they comment negatively about your boundaries. Remember, responding, instead of reacting, will allow you to glide past the negative energy and remain constructive.

- You're the only one in control of the energy in your life.

You're the master of your life, the one calling the shots. Every single interaction you have throughout the day carries negative or positive energy, and it's up to you to allow what is brought in to your personal space. Interacting with negative people shouldn't affect your entire day, and if it does, a situation that does affect your entire day is a red flag that your internal boundaries need some strengthening. Don't take others' negativity home with you.

- You must remember to be patient. Be patient not only with yourself as you begin to build new boundaries but also with others as they learn to respect your boundaries as well. If this concept of building and asking for respect of your boundaries is new to you, chances are it's also new to some others in your life as well.

- You need to respect others' boundaries just as you respect your own. Do you remember the chronic boundary violators I spoke of in the first chapter? That's not the direction we're moving toward. Be aware of others' noes, and simply learn to let some situations go.

The process of building boundaries with soul has no true end. I think it's safe to believe that there is not a single person who has completely mastered the skill of saying no or saying yes authentically. To me, we're all constantly growing, evolving, and learning about what makes us tick, and as long as we continue to evolve, our boundaries will consistently be challenged and questioned, both by ourselves and others. What is the most important, is the dialogue we continue to have with our higher self and our ego, and we must remain vigilant at tuning into the clues around the changes and shifts in our lives so that we can respond to each situation accordingly.

Remember, you already have the potential within you to live an authentic and fulfilled life. It's up to you to respect this potential, access it, and use it, and believe that you are worth living a life according to your rules.

Say no, but say yes just as much.

Build your boundaries with soul, and watch your life come into balance.

Starting today, I will strengthen my boundaries by:

Notes

YOUR JOURNEY HAS JUST BEGUN

To stay in touch with my boundary-building work, I encourage you to please become a member on my website. It's completely free! You can gain access to and save audio, written, and video posts, and inspirational sayings that will be both meaningful and helpful on your boundary-building journey.

HOW TO CONNECT WITH ME

Here are the ways you can get in touch with me:

- **Website:** CarleySchweet.com
- **Instagram:** @coachingbycarley
- **Facebook:** facebook.com/coachingbycarley
- **E-mail**: hello@coachingbycarley.com

HOW I CAN HELP

First and foremost, I am a mindfulness-based life coach. I help others build boundaries where they're needed most. I help overworked and undervalued men and women take back their time, quit people pleasing, and get back in touch with what it is they truly desire.

Consider signing up for one of my coaching programs—from private coaching, to group programs, to self-guided options, there's something for everyone.

THANK YOU

First and foremost, thank you to my family. Without you cheering me on, I wouldn't have the courage and strength to continue to do the work I pour my heart into each and every day. You all have been my biggest fans since day one, and I am forever grateful for your unwavering support. You know who you are!

This book was inspired by my experiences at the Institute for Integrative Nutrition (IIN), where I received my training in holistic wellness and health coaching.

IIN offers a truly comprehensive health-coach training program that invites students to deeply explore the things that are most nourishing to them. In teaching about the physical aspects of nutrition and eating wholesome foods that work best for each individual person and the concept of primary food—the idea that everything in life, including our spirituality, career, relationships, and fitness, contributes to our inner and outer health—IIN helped me reach optimal health and balance. My inner journey unleashed the passion that compels me to share what I've learned and inspire others.

Beyond teaching about personal health, IIN offers training in health coaching as well as business and marketing. Students who choose to pursue the field of health coaching professionally complete the program equipped with the communication skills and branding knowledge to create a fulfilling career encouraging and supporting others in reaching their own health goals.

With renowned wellness experts as visiting teachers and the convenience of their online learning platform, this school has changed my life, and I believe it will do the same for you. I invite you to learn more about IIN and explore how the health-coach training program can help you transform your life.

Feel free to contact me to hear more about my personal experience at CarleySchweet.com/integrativenutrition or call (844) 315-8546 to learn more.

A SMALL REQUEST

Did you enjoy my book? I would love a review! Please give me your honest feedback on Amazon by searching for Boundaries with Soul.

REFERENCES

1. Henry Cloud and John Townsend. *Boundaries*. (Running Press, 2004).

2. Justin Sonnenburg and Erica N Sonnenburg, "Gut Feelings–the 'Second Brain' in Our Gastrointestinal Systems [Excerpt]," Scientific American. May 1, 2015. Web: March 13, 2017.

3. Madeline Fry, "5 Signs That You Have Healthy Emotional Boundaries," Verily Magazine, July 11, 2016., accessed January 20, 2017. http://verilymag.com/2016/07/emotionally-open-healthy-boundaries-brene-brown-the-power-of-vulnerability-social-media-sharing.

48977566R00063

Made in the USA
San Bernardino, CA
09 May 2017